Points of Failure

20 Marketing Failures Destroying Your Profits and Growth Potential

with

Growing Your Business During an Economic Meltdown

by

Russ Holder

www.RussHolder.com

BEP Business Excellence Press

Points of Failure: 20 Marketing Failures Destroying Your Profits and Growth Potential

ISBN: 978-1-939315-17-5

Table of Contents

A Hostile Business Environment...1

Let's Get Real 2

Failure Point 1:
Not Understanding the Role of Marketing......................................11

Failure Point 2:
Not Understanding the E-Myth 15

Failure Point 3:
Not Utilizing the TriFecta of Business Growth 17

Failure Point 4:
Not Incorporating the Nine Growth Keys 21

Failure Point 5:
Not Having a Comprehensive Marketing Program 25

Failure Point 6:
Not Having a Unique Selling Proposition......................................31

Failure Point 7:
Not Understanding Your Customer's Lifetime Value 37

Failure Point 8:
Not Understanding the Cost of Losing a Customer 41

Failure Point 9:
Not Targeting Your Marketing..45

Failure Point 10:
Not Marketing "Inside" Before Going "Outside" 49

Failure Point 11:
Not Finding Your Perfect Price 53

Failure Point 12:
Not Using Direct Response Marketing 57

Failure Point 13:
Not Providing Enough Proof 63

Failure Point 14:
Not Reducing Risk 65

Failure Point 15:
Not Having a Proactive Referral Process 69

Failure Point 16:
Not Using the Internet to Your Advantage 71

Failure Point 17:
Not Having a Communication Plan...73

Failure Point 18:
Not Testing Your Marketing Activities 77

Failure Point 19:
Not Creating Marketing Systems 81

Failure Point 20:
Not Having an Exit Strategy...85

Conclusion: 87

Growing Your Business During an Economic Meltdown

Introduction 91

Living in Reality...95

USP/Differentiation 99

Understanding Business Growth 105

Creating a Business Growth Plan 117

Marketing in a Slow Economy...129

Recession Marketing Tips 133

Conclusion 145

About Russ Holder: 151

A Hostile Business Environment

Today's business world is evolving. Competition is fiercer than ever, the emergence of the Internet has changed the way many industries conduct business, and recessive economic conditions have forced many businesses to rethink their strategies.

As a business owner, entrepreneur or executive, you need real-world information to make intelligent decisions, and marketing is an area where so many bad decisions are made every day.

This book will introduce you to the most common marketing mistakes sabotaging business success and growth. Once able to recognize them, you'll see how prolific they are in your market, and you'll learn not only how to avoid them yourself, but how to make smarter marketing decisions that minimize your risk of failure.

Enjoy the book, and feel free to contact my office at (225) 308-3323 or visit me on the web at www.RussHolder.com if you have any questions.

Russ Holder

Let's Get Real

Let's start out with a realistic snapshot of our current business climate:

- More than 500,000 new businesses start each year (and that's not including 500,000 more home based, single operator businesses).

- 26,000 new products and brands are introduced each year.

- Overall, there is 50-80% more competition than 25 years ago.

- 70-80% of all businesses fail within their first five years in operation.

- 82-90% of businesses never see their 10th anniversary.

So why are businesses failing? The US Small Business Administration lists the following reasons why most small businesses fail as:

- Lack of capital.

- Poor management practices.

- Poor strategic planning.

- Failure to understand the market and market changes.

Those are pretty generic answers in my opinion. From what I've seen, most business failures are caused by four main reasons:

1. They don't have a real and unique competitive advantage in their market.

2. They are ineffective at communicating their value to their market.

3. Their business model doesn't work.

4. They are not in touch with their customers.

Don't make the mistake of thinking it's just small businesses that are failing. Companies that we thought would live forever have disappeared or faced bankruptcy.

- Lehman Brothers with $691 billion in revenue.

- Washington Mutual had $327.9 billion in revenue.

- Automobile manufacturers General Motors ($91 billion) and Chrysler ($39.3 billion).

- Wachovia Bank was considered "too big to fail" with over $812 billion in assets... sold to Wells Fargo for $12.7 billion.

- Countrywide Financial had $175 billion in assets, but had to sell to Bank of America for only $4 billion.

If you take a look at the Fortune 500 companies of 1980, you will find that 389 of them are no longer in business. This is sobering news for those of us with an entrepreneurial spirit.

Unfortunately, the bad news doesn't stop there:

- Customer acquisition costs have tripled over the last 20 years. Not only that, but…

- 20 years ago it took an average of 4 attempts to get in front of a buyer…

- Today it takes 8.4 attempts to get the same result, meaning…

- **It now costs 3 times more money to get half the results.**

With businesses spending six times as much money on customer acquisition, you would think they would have an endless supply of new customers and clients ready to do business with them. Unfortunately, the opposite is true.

The Biggest Problems in Business

According to a recent survey conducted by Entrepreneur Magazine, when asked about the biggest problems they face in their business, 92% of entrepreneurs gave one of the following four replies:

1. Difficulty generating or retaining customers (59.1%)
2. Not enough sales or orders.
3. Too many competitors.
4. Profit margins being squeezed.

Incredibly, **92% of the most pressing problems in small business are directly related to marketing.** Add to that the fact that customer acquisition costs are at an all-time high and it's easy to see that a new, more efficient approach to marketing is necessary to compete effectively in today's hostile marketplace.

Open your eyes and you will see it every day, in every media, and in every business: smart owners, executives and managers are not only making serious marketing mistakes, but they're failing at multiple levels. Of course they're not failing on purpose; they just don't realize that what they're doing (or not doing) is hurting their business.

You can call this ignorance or lack of knowledge. You can call it a lack of marketing savvy. No matter what you call it, ultimately it comes down to this: almost every business is making the same mistakes, and these mistakes result in massive losses in sales, profits, and customers.

Ponder this question for a moment: what does it take to make a business successful?

Many people think it's the product or service that makes the difference, but they're mistaken. In Des Plaines, IL in 1940 two hamburger restaurants opened. The first was Joe's Burgers, and it's still open today with sales of $1 million per year. The other was McDonald's, which is also still open today... with sales at $27 billion.

The first question I have for you is who do you think has the best burgers? I've never been to Joe's Burgers, so I really can't tell you whose burgers are better.

The second question is more important: who do you think has the best marketing and operating systems?

Entrepreneurs have a special place in my heart. These are people who put their dreams and livelihood into their businesses. They are passionate, driven, smart, and tend to be people who make things happen. It's unfortunate to see these people make important decisions without the proper information and planning.

Inferior products and services are purchased by consumers and businesses all the time, so success is not determined by quality. Smart people fail in business too often, so intelligence is not the key to success either.

A business only needs two things to succeed: customers and cash. Think about it... how many business problems can't be solved by increasing profitable sales?

The success and failure of almost every business comes down to one thing: how well it is marketed.

You might find this difficult to believe right now, but as you read through these marketing mistakes you'll understand that those who market most effectively win. That's why inferior products and services have stood the test of time, and it's why thousands of brilliant inventions fail. A good product or service is nothing without good marketing.

Marketing mistakes often equate to business failures. Ineffective marketing is why most businesses fail… or at least don't prosper as much as they should.

By directing your efforts on creating and implementing effective marketing in your business, you can make it immune to outside factors such as competition, and to an extent, a slow economy. Not only that, but the marketing failures so prevalent in today's marketplace represent an incredible opportunity for you. I promise you that your competitors are making many of the same mistakes listed in this book.

This book will give you an understanding of why they're failing. Not only will you learn to spot mistakes before they happen, but you will be able to transform them into winning and actionable strategies for your business.

Read through this book with both your business and your competition in mind. How are you (and they) doing in each of these areas?

It's important to understand that not all marketing mistakes are created equally. Some mistakes are deadly. Other mistakes just rob you of profits and keep you from producing maximum results. The key is that you catch them and stop doing them. If you don't act and keep doing the exact same thing, then you'll keep getting the same results.

This report will help you take control of your marketing, avoid crippling mistakes, and drive your business confidently into the future. You will discover how to identify these mistakes, make them right, and start producing the results you deserve.

There are three important things to note about this book. First of all, it's as much strategic as it is tactical. I could write a book about how to maximize the effectiveness of your marketing efforts, and it could make a big difference in your business, but I want to go beyond that to something much more important.

By directing your efforts on implementing effective marketing in your business, you can make it immune to outside factors such as competition and a slow economy.

If you want incredible and predictable results, you must think more strategically. You need to focus on creating marketing synergy and exponential growth, where the impact on your sales, profits, and market share are maximized.

The second note I want to make is about the order of these mistakes. The order is not coincidental. It is a result of combining the order of importance and logical sequencing.

Now let's get started.

Not Understanding the Role of Marketing

Let's start with the most fundamental question one could ask about business, and that's "what is the purpose of a business?" Here's how the "father of modern management", and perhaps the most important business mind of the 20th century, answers that question:

The Purpose of a Business

"Because its purpose is to create a customer, a business has two basic functions: marketing and innovation. Marketing and innovation produce results, all the rest are costs."

Peter Drucker
The Father of Modern Management

Okay, so what exactly is marketing? If you look at 10 different sources you'll probably get as many different definitions. Because of this let's focus less on the definition of marketing; rather, let's focus on the role of marketing in a business.

The purpose of marketing is to introduce and sell a company's products and services to new, present and past customers.

A business that is effective at marketing has the ability to consistently and repeatedly get customers and clients to purchase their products and services. They can sell and extract as much profit as ethically possible out of each customer over the lifetime of their relationship.

Marketing is leadership – leading a customer or client to do business with a company over and over again… for as long as possible.

Through understanding the role of marketing, we can see the importance of what happens after a new lead is generated or a new customer produced. A business must track and understand what is happening to a prospect immediately after inquiring about the company, product or service. If not, it's a huge mistake.

This mistake is greater if the right qualifying questions aren't asked, and salespeople spend time with the wrong prospects. What if the person answering the phone isn't saying the right things? What if the prospect isn't ready to buy at that moment, but may be ready at a later date? If the company isn't tracking this relationship and the prospect disappears, that's another mistake.

What if the deal is closed, the prospect becomes a customer, but is no longer included in the company marketing efforts? The customer will not buy as much as they could, and this is another massive mistake. And what if your service is poor, causing your customer to leave you for one of your competitors? Yes, that's right… another mistake.

By understanding what effective marketing is, it's easy to appreciate why businesses struggle. They haven't found ways to generate a constant stream of customers to keep buying from them.

Marketing should focus on all aspects of creating and maintaining customers and clients, and having a limited view of marketing, to that of just lead generation, customer acquisition or sales, is another major mistake. So many companies separate sales and marketing, often with the two departments not even communicating with each other. Selling is part of the marketing process, so never make the mistake of separating the two.

Failure Point 2:
Not Understanding "The E-Myth"

The E-Myth or the Entrepreneurial Myth, refers to a book by Michael Gerber entitled The E-Myth: Why Small Businesses Don't Work and What to Do About It. It is the all-time bestselling book on small business. I recommend that all business owners, executives, and aspiring entrepreneurs read it.

Although Gerber makes many great points in the book, I would like to focus on one of them specifically:

The E-Myth

"Most entrepreneurs fail because they spend too much time working IN their business, and not enough time working ON it."

Michael Gerber
Author of "The E-Myth"

Many business owners get caught up working IN their business, both as technicians or in dealing with day to day operations and putting out fires. They don't spend enough effort working ON the business, doing the things that will make it more successful and capable of growth.

Remember, marketing is one of only two business functions that are actual investments in your business. Unfortunately, it is also one of the most neglected business functions. Much of this neglect comes from exposure to bad information, and then making marketing decisions based on this bad information. Neglect also comes from not taking proper action.

Often busy executives rely on media reps for information and to "assist" them in creating their marketing programs and plans. This is a big mistake. Marketing is way too important for you to rely on outside entities with a vested interest in you using their media or other marketing vehicle. That doesn't mean that their tools aren't useful, it just means you need to properly educate and equip yourself to make sound marketing decisions.

Never let an outside source with a vested interest in you using their media or other marketing vehicle make marketing decisions for you.

Failure Point 3:
Not Utilizing the TriFecta of Business Growth

Ask almost any business owner for a description or copy of their marketing plan and you'll find that their plan is most often focused on lead generation. Lead generation can be conducted via many different media and methods, but the primary goal of that marketing is to get more new customers for the business.

Although getting new customers is necessary for any business to survive, it is almost always the most expensive form of marketing, and it's not the only goal your marketing should try to achieve.

There are only three ways to grow any business, and I call this the TriFecta of Business Growth. To get maximum growth results, all marketing programs should work to improve all three of these growth areas. When you are able to do this, something amazing happens to your business: You start to create and experience marketing synergy… and that gives you a great advantage in building and growing your business.

The majority of companies, including your competitors, only focus on one growth method, which is typically lead generation to increase the number of customers. This produces Linear Growth. If you increase the number of leads for a business by 10%, the business will grow by 10%.

The TriFecta of Business Growth

To maximize the efficiency and effectiveness of growing your business, management should always focus on the TriFecta of Business Growth:

1. Increase customer acquisition
2. Increase transaction values
3. Increase customer retention

When you focus your marketing efforts on the TriFecta of Business Growth, you put into effect the concept of Marketing Synergy.

Creating Marketing Synergy

When your marketing efforts focus on improving your business in all three growth categories, you can achieve what is called Geometric Growth. You introduce the concept of synergy, where the growth totals are greater than the sum of the individual parts.

If you are able to improve each of the three growth categories by 10%, your growth doesn't total up to 30%, it increases to 33.1% (see the diagram below). It's almost like you achieved a 3.1% growth bonus!

The TriFecta of Business Growth – 10% Improvements

	Number of Customers		Average Transaction Value		Yearly Purchase Frequency		Gross Sales
Now	1000	x	100	x	10	=	$1,000,000
+10%	1100	x	110	x	11	=	$1,331,000
					Actual Growth Achieved		**33.1%**

Note: In the following example I use improvements of 10% to make the calculations simple, and the growth improvements realistic. With a well-executed business development marketing program, some of those numbers could be much higher.

Properly utilizing the TriFecta of Business Growth allows you to start optimizing your marketing assets and eliminating waste in your marketing activities and budget. You will begin reducing your failures while gaining marketing momentum. No longer stuck in linear growth, you will have the freedom to think and plan more strategically, thus opening up many new marketing and business development options.

Business leaders should hold their marketing departments responsible for planning, measuring, and improving all three growth areas.

Monthly reports giving an accounting of your marketing's performance in all three areas should be required.

Failure Point 4:
Not Incorporating the Nine Growth Keys in Your Marketing

We just learned that all business growth falls under three primary categories, which I call the TriFecta of Business Growth. Now I want to introduce you to a concept that's even more exciting. When put into action in your business, this concept will give you almost unbelievable marketing synergy and exponential growth.

Let me ask you a question: How many different ways do you think there are to grow a business? You may be surprised to learn that there are just nine ways, each of those I call a Growth Key.

To maximize your business growth, your marketing efforts should focus on improving all Nine Growth Keys. By effectively accomplishing this with your marketing, you'll gain control over your sales and marketing processes. Not only does this get you infinitely closer to reaching your growth potential, it can be done more quickly than you might imagine.

Let me introduce you to the Nine Growth Keys of a business:

The Nine Growth Keys

Customer Acquisition:
1. Lead Generation
2. Conversion
3. Referrals

Customer Transactions:
4. Size of Purchase
5. Profit Margin

Customer Retention:
6. Buying Lifetime
7. Number of Purchases
8. Customer Attrition
9. Customer Reactivation

There are numerous proven strategies and tactics you can apply to massively improve each of these Nine Growth Keys. When you successfully combine the power of each growth key as a growth multiplier, you achieve maximum marketing synergy. You put the law of compounding to work for your business, and you gain the ability to grow to levels you never dreamed possible.

The Nine Growth Keys fit nicely into the TriFecta of Business Growth to form what I have named the TriFecta Exponential Growth Model.

TriFecta Exponential Growth Model™

Maximizing Marketing Synergy & Profitability

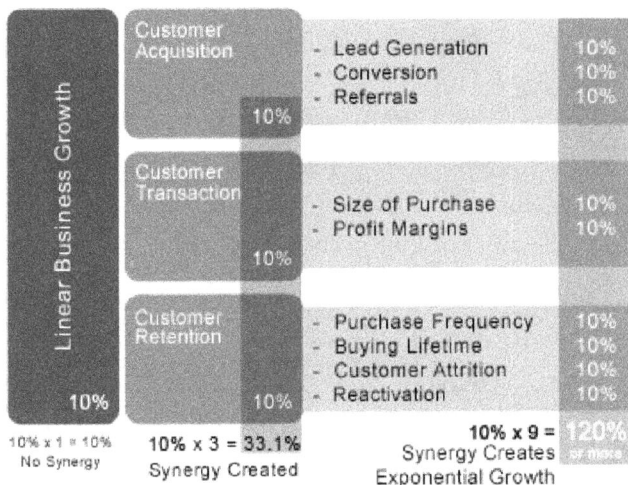

Linear Business Growth			
	Customer Acquisition 10%	- Lead Generation - Conversion - Referrals	10% 10% 10%
	Customer Transaction 10%	- Size of Purchase - Profit Margins	10% 10%
10%	Customer Retention 10%	- Purchase Frequency - Buying Lifetime - Customer Attrition - Reactivation	10% 10% 10% 10%
10% x 1 = 10% No Synergy	10% x 3 = 33.1% Synergy Created	10% x 9 = 120% Synergy Creates or more Exponential Growth	

The first column of the model represents how the majority of marketing plans are implemented, with a single focus of generating leads. A 10% improvement in lead generation equals a 10% growth in the company. This is Linear Growth.

The second column of the model puts the TriFecta of Business Growth to work for your business. You begin to achieve marketing synergy and Geometric Growth when you simultaneously improve all three growth areas (number of customers, average

23

transaction value, customer purchase frequency). Improvements of 10% in each of these areas results in a total of 33.1% growth, with marketing synergy producing bonus growth of 3.1% for your business.

The third column is where it gets incredibly exciting for business owners and executives. By improving each of the Nine Growth Keys, you are fully utilizing the Law of Compounding in growing your business, creating maximum marketing synergy. By improving each of the Nine Growth Keys by a mere 10%, you can grow your profits by 120-200% or more! That's the incredible power of the TriFecta Exponential Growth Model when put into action.

By successfully combining the power of each growth key as a growth multiplier, you gain the ability to achieve maximum marketing synergy, putting the concept of compounding and exponential growth to work for your business.

Failure Point 5:

Not Having a Comprehensive Marketing Program

At this point you have been introduced to the TriFecta Exponential Growth Model and how it integrates the TriFecta of Business Growth with the Nine Growth Keys. You can see how the law of compounding allows you to create incredible synergy among the growth keys to maximize your growth potential. Now it's time to put it to work for your business by creating a comprehensive marketing program built around the TriFecta Exponential Growth Model.

A Comprehensive Marketing Program is one that takes responsibility for improving all Nine Growth Keys, from lead generation through continually working toward extending your customer's buying lifetime. A Comprehensive Marketing Program does not allow customers to slip away from you. It doesn't leave anything out, because if you do, you reduce the effect the law of compounding has on your growth, and you destroy the synergy of the model.

Your marketing program should take responsibility for each of the Nine Growth Keys and the entire sales and marketing process.

There are many different marketing tools and tactics available, and the best marketing programs will have multiple tools working to achieve each one of the growth keys. You cannot rely on just one or two marketing tools for each of the growth keys. If you do, you are putting the growth and stability of your company at risk.

Let me give you an example using the growth key of lead generation…

Imagine that your business relies on television advertising to generate all of the leads for your business. What would happen if that media no longer produced results for you? What if it went out of business, or if one of your competitors started buying up huge chunks of air time, greatly reducing your visibility? It would definitely hurt, if not cripple, your business.

When building your business, redundancy is a key to stability. There are many factors in the marketplace that are out of your control. You are dependent upon vendors, media, sales people, etc., and these things can and will fail you from time to time. Not only must you have a contingency plan to deal with these situations, but you need to have redundant marketing tools and systems in place for every marketing function, thus minimizing the effects of failures.

What tools are you using now? Many small businesses only have a couple of tools working for them, and this mistake could lead to catastrophic failures. Having multiple marketing tools working for you to achieve each of the Nine Growth Keys is how you prevent marketing disaster.

You wouldn't believe how many people have told me that they've tried everything to grow their business, but nothing seems to work for them. Of course I respond by asking them what they are doing now, and what they have tried in the past.

Where I'm going with this is pretty clear. Their reply is often something like this: "I've tried the Yellow Pages, ran an ad in the paper, and I've sent out some direct mail letters."

I'm not saying that you can't have incredible success with any of those activities, because you can. Just think about what you could do by using 5, 10, or 20 more tools to grow your business? What effect would this have if each marketing tool was working for you and producing a positive return on investment? This is the key to creating multiple streams of income, and it's what every business should strive to achieve. There are literally hundreds of different marketing tools and strategies that you can put to work for your business. How many are you using to your advantage right now?

When evaluating new marketing opportunities for your business, ask yourself which growth keys the activity will help you improve. Many marketing tools can impact multiple growth keys when used properly. Two that come to mind are sales people and company newsletters.

A sales person can accomplish every growth key on their own. If you don't have other marketing tools supporting the growth and stability of your company, make certain that the duties of your sales people include all Nine Growth Keys. For the sake of efficiency I don't recommend this practice. Use your sales team to achieve the growth keys that will generate return, and that's closing deals. Most often they are the best tool for accomplishing this growth key.

The company newsletter has incredible utility in marketing. Through education and follow up, it assists in conversion, generating referrals, increasing frequency of purchases, extending a customer's buying lifetime, reducing customer attrition, and reactivating inactive customers. I'm giving you a great tip here: you should be using a company newsletter. Every business needs one.

I'll repeat this because it's important: **to achieve maximum growth and stability you need a marketing program with multiple marketing tools constantly improving each of the Nine Growth Keys.**

In the city where I live, I know of two businesses that are constantly testing new media and marketing opportunities. In all honesty, their marketing isn't very good, and there are many things they could do to improve the results they get. But I want to give them credit. They understand the importance of marketing, and they understand the importance of testing new marketing activities. Even though they have immense room for improvement, both of them have the most successful businesses of their category in our local marketplace. Good for them.

Failure Point 6:

Not Having a Unique Selling Proposition

This is by far the most common marketing mistake in business, and the most detrimental.

The Unique Selling Proposition (USP) is the one thing that differentiates you or your business from your competitors in the minds of your clients and prospects. Your USP is what makes the difference between having a truly outstanding business or a faltering one. **Not being able to clearly differentiate your business from competitors or other options available to your market is a huge marketing mistake, and the demise of many businesses.**

Some businesses have a USP and don't even know it. When they can find a way to identify their USP then quickly and powerfully present it in their sales and marketing messages, they begin to stand out in their crowded marketplace.

The ability to articulate a strong USP is the single most important strategic advantage you will ever have, and I can't stress enough how important this is to you. How can you expect your clients or customers to choose you over the other options available to them if they can't see what makes you unique and beneficial to them?

There have been many outstanding businesses founded on a USP alone. The most famous example is Dominos' Pizza. Tom Monahan made Domino's Pizza one of the most successful fast food businesses in the world with the strength of the USP "Red hot pizza delivered to your door in 30 minutes or less – guaranteed." This USP guaranteeing delivery propelled Dominos' Pizza from a start-up to a 4 billion dollar company in just a few years. Now many pizza restaurants can deliver you a pizza in 30 minutes. It's no longer unique, and Domino's no longer rules the pizza delivery category.

Here's a couple of other great USPs:

- FedEx has the 'confidence inspiring' USP of "When it absolutely, positively has to be there overnight."

- And another great one is the USP from Lens Crafters: "Helping people see better one hour at a time."

What is your USP? If you think it's "good quality" or "good service", I hate to tell you this, but that won't cut it. It has to be more specific than that, and if possible, quantitative.

If you're unclear about what your USP may be, listen to the top salesperson in your company. It is often instinctive for them to sell what the customers really want. Hopefully the company can deliver.

Competition is the most important aspect of your USP. If your competition is doing it, it's not a USP because it's not unique.

Of course your USP must be very important to your customers and clients. You could have the most unique product in the world, but if your customers don't care about it, that uniqueness carries little value.

The USP is the most important part of any marketing plan. The process of creating your USP often identifies which target markets should be pursued, as it is the central concept and foundation of all the marketing and sales efforts of a company.

Putting Your USP to Use

Often a company can uncover or create a decent USP, but they fail to integrate it successfully into their marketing efforts. Many USPs are ineffective because the sales team is not on board. A sales presentation designed around a strong USP can increase conversion rates significantly.

Business executives must require teams and departments to make their USP an integral part of their sales and marketing processes. From placing advertisements, your marketing communications, sales scripts and presentations, the USP needs to be anchored in all sales and marketing activities and any ongoing communications with customers.

To get you started on identifying and creating a USP, here are a few questions to ask yourself:

- Who is your target market?

- What are the three most important results they want from the purchase of your product or service?

- What are three reasons why your best customers do business with you over your competition?

- What are the main problems of your target market as they relate to your product or service?

- How do you uniquely solve their problems?

Now try to distill the information from your responses to these five questions into a powerful and concise statement.

A couple of important notes before I close on USPs:

- Depending on their different revenue sources, a company may have more than one USP.

- USPs change (remember the Domino's Pizza example) and need to be evaluated on a regular basis. Again, the key factor in changing a USP is what the competition is doing.

If your market views your company as the same as your competitors, what do you think becomes the most important criteria when they want your products and services? That's right, price.

Creating and integrating a USP into your company is one of the best ways to remove your business out of "price wars."

Do not dismiss the importance of the USP. The commitment to create and implement a strong USP is the single most common reason why I see otherwise good marketing fail.

Take a look at your competition. I can almost guarantee they don't have a USP. By creating and integrating a USP into your business you gain a competitive edge that will make a massive difference in capturing market share from your competitors.

Failure Point 7:

Not Understanding Your Customer's Lifetime Value

One of the biggest mistakes I see companies make is basing marketing decisions on one-time purchase results of a customer, not the lifetime value of a customer.

For example, to attract new customers a retail store runs an advertisement that costs $1,500. The ad generates 10 new customers that purchased an average of $100 each, totaling $1,000 in new sales.

The store interprets the results of the promotion as $1,500 ad cost minus $1,000 in sales, equals a $500 loss. They conclude that the advertisement didn't work for them... And that's a big mistake.

The retail store is failing to see the future opportunity for more purchases. If this store has great products and good customer service, let's say, on average, those 10 new customers come back twice a year and spend $100 each time. On top of that, let's assume that they will continue doing business with this store for an average of 5 years each. Now we're looking at 20 return visits and purchases for $100 each, or a total of $2,000. Multiply that times the 5 years that these customers will stay with you and you receive a total value of $10,000 generated from this $1,500 mailing. The lifetime value of those 10 customers is $10,000, and that's not including any referrals they send to the store.

The Lifetime Customer Value is the average profit a customer generates over the duration of their relationship with a business.

In determining the Lifetime Customer Value for your business, a good guide to start with is using 5 years for the duration of time a customer does business with you. However, to make the most accurate business and marketing decisions you need to figure out the exact number.

Use this simple calculator to determine the Lifetime Customer Value for your business:

Lifetime Customer Value Calculator		
Dollar value of your average transaction:	$	
Number of transactions per year:	X	
Average annual revenue per customer:	$	
Average number of years per customer:	X	
Lifetime revenue per average customer:	$	
Average profit margin:	%	
Average Lifetime Customer Value:	$	

To give you a successful example of an industry that understands this concept well, let's look at DVD and CD clubs. For only $1.00 you can get 5 Free DVDs delivered to your door. Obviously it costs the company much more than that to send them the 5 DVDs.

These DVD and music clubs are savvy marketers that understand the lifetime value of a new customer. They have calculated the average amount of time a customer continues to do business with them, and they know there will be additional orders that more than make up for the loss on the first order.

This lifetime value process is the same information used by manufacturers in determining whether to purchase a piece of equipment. Up front they may not cover their costs, but over the lifetime of the equipment the return justifies their investment. You should think about marketing in the exact same way.

A shift in your thinking can give you incredible leverage in marketing your business. When you know your Lifetime Customer Value, you learn that you can actually spend more money to acquire customers. This gives you a great advantage over competitors in your marketplace because it allows you to think more strategically about growing your business.

Failure Point 8:
Not Understanding the Cost of Losing a Customer

Along with understanding your Lifetime Customer Value, it's important to have a clear grasp of the real effects losing a customer has on your business.

One lost and unhappy customer or client can have a far-reaching impact on your business, because negative word-of-mouth travels faster and further than positive word-of-mouth. By understanding this concept, you realize that you're not only losing their business, but you lose the business of their potential referrals.

If an unhappy customer were to tell 10 other people about their experience (or not refer those 10 people to do business with you), and each of those 10 people told 5 others, the total number of people affected by that one bad experience would be 61 (see calculations on the following page).

If 25% of those people choose not to do business with you because of this negative word-of-mouth, that totals 15.25 people.

If each of those 15.25 customers had similar buying habits as your original customer, the lifetime revenues lost can be astronomical.

Here is a calculator to illustrate this example using a Lifetime Customer Value of $1,500:

Cost of Losing a Customer	
The original unhappy "lost" customer:	1
Tells 10 others about the experience:	10
Who each tell 5 others:	50
Total people knowing of bad experience:	61
25% don't buy because of negative word-of-mouth:	15.25
Average Customer Lifetime Value:	$1,500
Total lost income from one bad experience:	$22,875

Total lost income from one bad experience: $22,875.

Maybe you're having a hard time believing those figures, so let's cut those numbers in half to $11,437.50. That's still difficult to come to terms with, so let's cut it in half again. You still have a total of $5,718.75 lost, and that's a lot of money for letting one person leave unhappy.

Failure Point 9:
Not Targeting Your Marketing

Just as you can't be all things to all people, you can't market your products and services to everyone, even if you think that everyone needs them.

I'm not saying that you can't be successful doing this. What I am saying is that you greatly reduce your efficiency and potential by not focusing on select groups of consumers or businesses. These specific groups are called "niches."

What groups of people or businesses are more likely to want and need your products and services? What niches are most likely to be able to afford your products and services? There's no point in targeting them if they can't afford to buy from you.

People often ask me, "If I limit my market, won't I be reducing my chances of doing business with more customers?"

Of course you will, but by targeting your marketing to niches you are able to connect with them at much higher levels. To succeed in today's hyper-competitive marketplace you need to concentrate your marketing resources on smaller, well-chosen segments or niches. This results in higher conversion rates and lower customer acquisition costs.

Niche marketing represents your best chance of getting a good return on your marketing investment.

Which Accountant Would You Choose?

Imagine you just started a new restaurant and you need an accountant. You do a Google search for accountants in your local area and see several descriptions in the search results, such as the following:

Generic Accounting Services – tax preparation, auditing, bookkeeping, payroll services, help for start-ups, management accountants, etc.

Restaurant Accounting Services – specializing in helping restaurants get their businesses running quickly, efficiently, and profitably.

Which accounting firm are you likely to choose? Of course this example is obvious, but it serves to show how effective niche marketing can be. It's unfortunate that so few businesses follow this simple approach to marketing.

You are able to specifically market to the needs and requirements of your chosen niche. You are telling them that 'you are the company that knows them and their situation better than anyone else.'

When you focus on smaller groups you may not get the business of others outside of your targeted group. However, what actually happens is that you increase the amount of business you receive from your target group or niche.

By concentrating on niche markets, you can become a dominant force because your products and services are seen as "specifically designed" to solve the problems of a particular market. This dynamic can help you achieve high market share in a particular category very quickly.

Not focusing on specific niche markets is one of the most common of all marketing mistakes.

Failure Point 10:
Not Marketing "Inside" Before Going "Outside"

I mentioned earlier in this book that the majority of businesses focus their marketing efforts on lead generation, looking outside of their business for growth. When I use the word "outside", I mean using traditional marketing resources for lead generation activities. This can include advertising, trade shows, internet marketing, sales team prospecting, direct mail, etc.

The minute a prospect inquires about your products or services, they become "inside" the company. This is where real marketing takes over.

These prospects have entered the sales process of the company. They are having sales conversations, being exposed to sales pitches, and talking with technical experts to discover if your solution is best for them.

This is the typical sales process for most businesses: lead generation – lead qualification – solution presentation – close the deal. Many things can go wrong within this process:

- The wrong leads are being generated.

- The presentation being made is not being done well.

- The prospects are not being closed as effectively as possible.

- And after the close, there may not be an on-going process of marketing to these customers.

What is happening "inside" the company is just as important to your profitability, if not more important, than what is going on "outside" to generate more leads.

This approach to marketing is more non-traditional than what most advertising and marketing agencies like to push. They make their money convincing you that the answer for more sales is in the creation of more prospects.

The tendency to focus marketing efforts on lead generation and prospecting will reduce your ability to achieve maximum growth for your business.

When you put the TriFecta Exponential Growth Model and Nine Growth Keys to work for your business, you find there is often a tremendous amount of waste with "inside" marketing processes, and you're literally throwing away many of the leads you generate. Significant sales and profits are often found without having to spend more money to generate new leads.

Very often the most efficient way for a business to market themselves is to optimize their sales process and eliminate all the areas of waste. After this is done, more resources can be directed toward lead generation because you have effective systems in place to convert prospects into customers, and to maximize the Customer Lifetime Value, thus creating maximum profit opportunity for the business.

Failure Point 11:

Not Finding Your Perfect Price

The majority of businesses are not charging the right prices for their products and services. Consider how most people arrive at their price:

- By looking at what your competitors charge (actually, many people don't even do this simple step).

- By deciding "where" you want your customers to see you – as "low-priced", "middle-of-the-road", or "high-end."

- You then price your product or service based on the results of the two above points.

This is what is known as "price positioning", and to a certain extent it does serve a purpose. However, it means that you base your prices on where you see yourself positioned in the marketplace in relation to what your competitors charge.

There's a big fundamental mistake in doing this. People rarely buy on price alone. There is a small percentage of people who strictly buy on price, who buy the cheapest no matter what, but they are a minority.

As a rule, people automatically value your product or service more if you charge a higher price, unless, of course, what you're selling is viewed as a commodity. If you charge too low, your prospects will think that you can't be very good. If you charge high prices, you must make certain your clients receive excellent value from you, because that's what they expect.

It's nearly impossible for you to determine how much people are willing to pay you for your products and services. You could be lucky and guess the right price, but it's not likely. You're looking for the price point that gives you the biggest profit, not necessarily the greatest revenue, over the lifetime of your relationship with that customer.

You must let your customers and clients decide what the perfect price is, and the only way you can do this is by testing. In simple terms this means having one price for the first 10 prospects, another price for the next 10, and another price for the next 10. Then you can calculate which price gives you the greatest profit.

Don't make the mistake of thinking that the highest price always wins, because you may find many more people buy at a lower price point, translating into more money because you acquire more customers.

Too many companies don't take the time or effort to differentiate themselves and add considerable value to their offering. Without developing and promoting their uniqueness (their USP), they become a commodity and the only way they can compete is on price.

When you learn how to add substantially more value than your competitors, then you can charge a premium for your product and service offerings.

Again, some people are only after the cheapest price they can find, but let me ask you a couple of questions: Are those the customers and clients you want? Are they customers that are likely to stay with you for a long time?

Hopefully you answered "no" to both of those questions.

Pricing is often the quickest and easiest way to generate new profits in your business, and you'll be amazed at what you can charge if you start adding value to your offering with tactics such as risk reversal, proof and premiums.

Failure Point 12:
Not Using Direct Response Marketing

The investment required for successful media advertising can be very high for small and medium-size businesses. Often entrepreneurs and business executives give media advertising a shot, but find they don't get any return on their investment. They end up frustrated and quit.

The most common reason why most businesses fail with advertising is because they are doing the wrong type of advertising. They are doing Institutional Advertising instead of Direct Response Advertising. Media sales reps and advertising agencies sell them on the concept to advertise for "branding" purposes. They are told that if they don't advertise, then their competitors will beat them to their customers.

I'm not going to argue this statement, because it could possibly be true. However, it is not necessarily true.

I recommend to all small and medium-size businesses that all of their advertising should be direct response. The purpose of direct response is to do just that: direct a response of some kind. This response can be in the form of a purchase from your store, a request for more information or a free consultation, etc. Because the purpose is to generate a response of some kind, direct response advertising can be measured and held accountable for results.

The majority of advertising that you see in any media is institutional advertising, and it doesn't ask for any instant or direct response. These ads often look exactly the same as all the other ads: the company name is the headline of the ad, there is very little copy on the ad, lots of "white" space, and no incentive to call now.

If your ads look like this, do yourself a favor and stop running them now! You are wasting your money.

Institutional or image advertising is fine if all you want to do is promote the image of a company… but it doesn't generate sales.

Considering that your prospects and customers don't really care about you, your business, or what you sell (all they care about is how you can help them), image or institutional advertising is a waste of money.

Institutional advertising can help build brand awareness, and this is important for large companies like Coca-Cola and Nike who have enormous advertising budgets. Most small and mid-size businesses, however, cannot afford to spend their money this way.

Think of your advertising as a sales person.

Would you hire someone to go door-to-door handing out business cards? The card has your company name, address, phone number, and hopefully what you sell is made evident somewhere on the card via a company name or slogan. If this sales person were paid a base salary, wouldn't you agree that this would be a waste of money, and that you should find a better rep who will do a little more "selling?"

That's exactly what institutional advertising is. It's a sales rep saying "Hi, I'm with Acme Widget Company. Call me if you need widgets." Just as you would demand more from your sales reps, you should demand more from your advertising.

After all, wouldn't you prefer a sales person (or advertising effort) that generates immediate leads and sales? Or would you prefer a sales person (or advertising effort) that builds your brand awareness in hope that sometime in the future someone who wants your product or service will remember your company and may or may not buy from you?

Components of a Good Direct Response Ad

- Powerful, benefit laden headlines and subheadings
- Lots of copy written in a personal style
- A powerful offer
- Your Unique Selling Proposition
- Sells the benefits
- Testimonials
- A reason to respond immediately
- A free bonus for responding
- Reply mechanisms
- Advertisement response is measureable, and you can hold the ad accountable for results.

There are many great books and resources on writing direct response ads, and I suggest you read several of them.

Start running ads that direct an immediate response that you can monitor, track and test. Institutional advertising merely tells your market (if they pay attention to it) that your company is there, so you cannot measure results. While the expense of the ad is real, the return on investment is unknown, and probably almost nothing.

Failure Point 13:
Not Providing Enough Proof

If you've ever been a sales person, you know that selling isn't easy. Unless you can convince your prospect that your product or service will give them the result they need, you won't get the sale. Worse than that, people are more skeptical today than ever, so what you say to your prospects is often not believed or internalized.

How can you prove to your prospects that you can deliver on your promises? It's actually easier than most people think: offer proof.

By not using proof, companies are making the sales and marketing processes much more difficult than necessary. Simple tools such as testimonials, success stories, pictures, statistics, customer lists, physical demonstrations, etc., are easy to use and can have an incredible impact on conversion rates.

With proof, quantity and quality are both important. The key point to remember is that **you should include as much proof as you possibly can into your sales and marketing processes.**

Failure Point 14:
Not Reducing Risk

For your customers, the benefit of your product or service is gained after the sale is made. Sometimes it can take days, weeks, months, and even years for them to realize the benefits. This makes the transaction with your company a risky one for the customer, and it is this risk that often prevents a customer from buying from you.

Just as providing your prospects proof that your product or service performs as promised, creating ways to remove or reduce the risk of the transaction will make them more inclined to buy from you. This process is called risk reversal, and it can have an incredible effect on your business success.

Risk reversal is simply removing barriers of entry away from the prospect, and ensuring that they keep progressing toward the sale. The most common type of risk reversal is the guarantee, and the best type of guarantee is one that guarantees a specific result or benefit.

A company that reverses risk and guarantees results gains an incredible competitive advantage in their marketplace, and they will be rewarded with more business. In fact, a risk reversal policy can be a very strong Unique Selling Proposition (USP) in itself. Entire businesses (and very successful ones) have been built around the USP of risk reversal.

By Adding Risk Reversal to Your Business, You Will...

- Convert a higher percentage of prospects into customers and clients.
- Differentiate your business from competitors.
- Add value to your offering, resulting in prospects and customers appreciating you more.

If you've given thought to the concept of guarantees and risk reversal in your business, I know what question has come to your mind...

"What about all the people that will take advantage of, and abuse, my risk reversal policy or guarantee?"

One of the keys to successful risk reversal is to offer a great product or service. When you do, the return and refunds will be minimal. Yes, there will be the occasional customer that will abuse your offer, but the increased sales you gain from risk reversal will greatly outweigh any returns. If you are failing to use a risk reversal strategy in your business, then you're not getting all the business you could.

Failure Point 15:
Not Having a Proactive Referral Process

If you have a good product or service, then you should receive referrals or recommendations from your clients and customers. The better you are, the more unsolicited referrals you should get.

However, if you want to get many times more referrals than you're currently getting, then you need to create a proactive referral process and system. This is something that very few businesses do, and it's causing them to miss out on many of their ideal customers.

Referral systems don't have to be complex. They can be as simple as asking your client or customer for the names of three people just like them who would be interested in receiving some information and a special offer from you. I doubt this method gives you the best results possible, but if you don't have a proactive system in place to generate referrals, I promise you that it will greatly improve your current results.

In case you haven't thought about it, referral business should be your favorite type of business. You rarely have to compete on price, the closing process is usually much faster and more efficient, and these customers tend to be ones that you'll enjoy working with.

Think about this: **if you got just one referral from 50% of your clients or customers every year, what sort of difference would that make to your business?** Actually, you would grow your customer base by 50% every year, and your business would double in less than two years.

Failure Point 16:
Not Using the Internet to Your Advantage

The internet offers a wonderful opportunity for small businesses because it has leveled the playing field between large companies and small companies more than any other technology in history. It's a costly mistake for most small businesses to not have a website and not use the internet properly.

In the United States, internet penetration is now over 74%, and the number of high-speed internet users almost doubles every year. The internet is also prominent in other continents, with over 450 million users in Asia, 340 million in Europe, and 130 million in Latin America. With these numbers growing every year, there could be an opportunity for any company to sell their products and services over the web.

The purpose of this report is to identify major failures in marketing, and the internet is an opportunity that many small and local businesses haven't learned how to take advantage of. As long as you're not properly using the internet, you are failing to reach your potential.

If you have a static website that serves as an "online brochure", I encourage you to open your mind to the possibility of generating leads and using your website to advance prospects and customers through the process of doing business with you.

I have created a special report titled *Make the Internet Work for Your Local Business*, and it covers the potential the internet offers and how to use it to your advantage. Although it is written for local businesses, the concepts and principles apply to just about any small or medium-size business that would like to make the internet a profit center. Just contact my office via email or phone, and we'll get a copy to you right away.

Failure Point 17:
Not Having a Customer Communication Plan

How often do you keep in touch with your customers and prospects? If your answer is less than once per month, then this is a marketing mistake severely limiting your profits.

You must make an effort to keep in touch with your prospects, customers and clients because...

- You want to get as much profit out of them as ethically possible by selling more products and services to them.

- You want to keep your customers for as long as possible.

- Timing is a critical factor in marketing and sales. Just because someone isn't interested in buying your products and services today, it doesn't mean they won't be interested in the future.

Keeping in touch with customers and clients is one of the simplest and most important marketing activities you will ever use, so don't take this lightly. Do this one thing and your sales will increase.

"An increase in customer retention of 5% can yield an increase of profit of 25-85%.

Frederick Reiccheld
Author of "The Loyalty Effect"
Harvard Business Review Press

Smart business builders understand the importance of marketing for customer retention, not just customer acquisition. Since it costs up to 5 times more to obtain new customers than retain ones you already have, this is a very intelligent strategy.

A properly implemented customer communication program will help you:

- Improve customer retention

- Increase referral generation

- Increase customer frequency of purchase

- Reactivate past customers and clients

- Educate prospects and customers about the benefits you provide

- Extend customer buying lifetime

- Differentiate your business from competitors

Keeping in touch can and should be done via several different marketing tools. You should not depend on just one marketing tool or tactic for this important task. Phone calls, newsletters, direct mail and email can all be used very inexpensively, and when used together, create incredible synergy.

Considering everything that a strong communication plan can do for your business, it is foolish not to have a communication program that reaches your customers and prospects every month.

Failure Point 18:

Not Testing Marketing Activities Before Rolling Them Out

One of the most powerful marketing concepts you'll ever discover is also one of the most ignored: Testing is the key to maximizing your profits and minimizing losses. Companies that take the time to properly test their marketing efforts can easily double their effectiveness.

Consider this: if a sales presentation, advertisement, direct mail letter, postcard, or any other marketing activity isn't working, try something different. It's a pretty simple and logical concept.

The key to testing is to pay close attention to what you change so you can understand what changes work best. In fact, when testing only make one change at a time. If an ad you're running isn't working for you, don't start over from scratch. Try just changing the headline, or the placement. Make small changes and monitor the results. You're searching for the variable that causes change and increases response. If you test ten things at once, you'll never know which change worked.

If you don't test, you'll never get the best results or return on your marketing investment. Additionally, testing helps you reduce the risk of failure with a marketing activity. Before you ever invest any significant amount of time, effort or money in any marketing or promotional effort, test the effectiveness of your campaign. If it doesn't work out the way you want it to, you haven't wasted unnecessary resources.

Two of the most important elements to test are the headlines of your ads and marketing pieces, and the offers you make to prospects. With my clients I have seen headline changes increase advertisement response rates by 300% and even 700%.

Another client of mine had a specialized consulting practice in the telecom industry. By changing his offer we were able to improve his closing ratio from 20% to over 60%. That's an improvement of 300%. And that is the incredible power of testing.

Always test small before making major commitments to a product, service, or marketing campaign. You will never really know what works best until you test.

Failure Point 19:
Not Creating Marketing Systems

Of the hundreds of businesses I've consulted with, I can count on one hand how many times I have seen a business with any sales and marketing systems in place. What I almost always find is haphazard and inconsistent marketing and ineffective sales caused by the omission of a structured system or process.

It shouldn't surprise you to learn that sales and marketing must work hand-in-hand, both relying on each other for support. Your goal should be to create a sales and marketing machine. You could be the top expert in your field with the best product or service imaginable, but you will never maximize the growth of your business unless you master sales and marketing.

As mentioned earlier in this book, inferior products and services thrive because they are marketed and sold effectively. Conversely, when superb products and services fail, it can almost always be attributed to the business failing at sales and marketing.

I know you think your business is different, everybody does. Let me ask you two simple questions:

- Do you need profitable clients and customers?
- Once you have them, do you need to keep them buying from you?

In these two ways every business is the same. They need a steady supply of customers and clients, and they need to keep them to maximize profits throughout the duration of the relationship.

Whether you're an accounting firm or a manufacturer, acquiring and keeping customers involves the same set functions. That's why no matter what product or service you sell, you're in the "sales and marketing" business.

Marketing Systems You Need to Have

For almost all businesses there are several functions of marketing that must be mastered to maximize growth:

- Lead generation
- Prospect education
- Prospect conversion
- Referral generation

- Customer retention

- Continually monitoring and satisfying customer needs

- Maintaining customer relationships and building loyalty.

- Reactivating inactive customers

Regardless of the products and services you sell, optimizing and systematizing these functions will help you achieve your business potential.

You should strive to systematize all of your sales and marketing activities. Systems are reliable and predictable. You can turn on an effective system and predict what results you will get. You can also turn off a system if you ever need to. When done properly, systems allow you to put your sales and marketing efforts on "autopilot" and move on to creating and implementing your next marketing activity.

Failure Point 20:
Not Having an Exit Strategy

One of the worst mistakes entrepreneurs make is not building their business with the end in mind. **The ambition of every business owner should be to sell their business at the highest possible price in the shortest possible time.** Even if selling your business is not your goal, having this mindset makes a huge impact on your success.

At some point in time you will be getting out of your business. Maybe you'll sell your business and move on to something else, or maybe you'll just want to retire from actively running your business. Sometimes people fall on hard times and lose their business, and other times people die and leave their business for someone else to operate.

You never know when you may need to get out of your business, or what circumstances may arise that may cause you to leave. Therefore, one of your goals should be to make your business "investor ready" so you can cash out when you want or need to, and for the amount of money you need or want to get out of your business.

In itself, your business is a product. It's up to you to make certain it's a product built to sell and one that is increasing in asset value. You need to begin thinking about your business as an asset you own that will be worth a tremendous amount of money someday.

When you approach your business the right way, you are building a sellable asset. When approached the wrong way, your business is merely a job... something you derive income from. Think about it like this: you can work for your business and the money you get from it with nothing to show for it in the end, or you can work for the same amount of time and have an asset you can sell for a multiple of profit.

When you build your business using the TriFecta Exponential Growth Model and the Nine Growth Keys, you are adding to the value of your business. Sure, you'll grow in profits and market share, but you'll also continually test, measure, and systematize your marketing processes. All of these factors add to the value of your business and add to your exit strategy opportunities.

Conclusion

As you've discovered throughout this book, business owners and executives make many mistakes with their sales and marketing efforts. The good news is that with an intelligent and systematic approach toward growing your business, you can create an unstoppable marketing machine with many powerful competitive advantages within your marketplace.

That's why I wrote the book *Maximizing Business Growth: Your Fast Track Guide for Achieving Exponential Growth in Any Economy*. With the purpose of creating massive marketing synergy and exceptional business growth, you will learn how to put the TriFecta Exponential Growth Model to work for you by creating a comprehensive business development and marketing program focused on the Nine Growth Keys. Doubling your sales, profits and market share can be easier than you ever imagined.

The foundation and principles of the TriFecta Exponential Growth Model have made billions of dollars for businesses of all sizes. But principles are not enough... you must know how to execute all aspects of your marketing program flawlessly to get breakthrough results.

I wish you success in all of your business endeavors, and feel free to contact me if I can be of assistance to you in your efforts to maximize the growth of your business.

Russ Holder

Office Phone: (225) 308-3323

Email: Russ@RussHolder.com

Web: Russ@RussHolder.com

Growing Your Business During an Economic Meltdown

How to Survive and Thrive During a
Recession and Other Hostile Environments

by

Russ Holder

www.RussHolder.com

Introduction

How would you like to learn the secrets of producing incredible growth in your business? To not only take your business to the next level in sales, profits and market share, but to catapult it light years ahead of where you are now, and light years ahead of your competition.

And how would you like to rid yourself and your business of cold calling and unsuccessful advertising? To learn how to bring in more customers in a few months than you previously did in an entire year... so you can stop chasing prospects and get them to start contacting you.

Impossible you say? Well believe me, it's not. So if you're a business owner, manager, a professional, or an entrepreneur. In fact, if you're any person who is responsible in any way of attracting new customers or clients to your organization, this audio program is for you.

It doesn't matter if you're in the manufacturing business, if you sell an intangible or professional service, or if you sell a future vision or dream. It doesn't matter if your business is home based, or if it's a corporation, an association, or somewhere in between.

If the idea of learning the secrets of achieving exponential growth in your business sounds exciting to you, then you will enjoy this audio program. You're about to learn some of the latest, most important concepts, strategies and techniques that can absolutely change the way you do business... in fact, it will change the way you WANT to do business.

So let me introduce you to Russ Holder. Russ is the owner of TriFecta Marketing, a consulting firm specializing in business development marketing. He is also the author of TriFecta Marketing Machine: Achieving Exponential Growth in Your Business... Even in a Slow Economy. Russ is going to reveal to you some of the most powerful strategies and techniques he has used to help hundreds of small and mid-sized businesses achieve and eclipse their growth goals.

Through his consulting, coaching and training programs, Russ has helped Fortune 500, Inc. 500, and over 150 businesses in dozens of industries achieve amazing growth while adding incredible profits to their bottom line through his business development marketing programs.

There's no fluff or filler in this program; just good, solid and useable information. Information that can help you grow your business faster, easier, and more profitably than ever before. Information that has helped large corporations, associations, and even small businesses gain a decided advantage in their respective markets.

And if you'll take the time to understand and apply these concepts to your business, you can't help but succeed in the same way countless others have. And remember how in my opening statement I asked if you would like to learn the secrets of producing incredible growth in your business? You're not only going to learn these things, you're going to get dozens of ideas, concepts, strategies and techniques that you can begin using right away in your business.

So grab a pen and a notepad and get ready for an experience that can literally change the way you look at and conduct business.

Living in Reality

Contrary to popular belief, building and growing a successful business that commands a dominating position in your marketplace doesn't have to be incredibly difficult or costly.

Now it's true, today's often hostile business environment is more competitive than ever before, in almost every industry or profession. But there is also more opportunity... especially for those business owners and managers that understand a few vital business development principles and key marketing concepts.

It doesn't really matter if you run a large corporation, or if you run a one-person, home-based business, there are only a handful of things you need to master to gain an incredible advantage in your marketplace.

This year an unbelievable amount of businesses, both large and small, will close their doors forever. Analysts have differing opinions as to why so many businesses fail, with one popular opinion being a lack of capital, or underfunding.

Another common opinion for failure is because of poor business management practices. And other say that some businesses are started by the wrong people… that they lack entrepreneurial skills and would be better off working IN their business as a technician or employee, rather than running the business themselves.

But when you get right down to it, for that business to be in business in the first place, that business must have only one thing… and that's customers. You see, creating customers is the purpose of every business.

Think about it this way… you can have all the funding in the world… you can have great management skills, and you can have an incredible entrepreneurial mind-set. But unless you have customers to purchase your products and services in sufficient numbers, you'll never have a successful business.

The Reality of Business Failure

So here's the reality of business failure: most businesses fail because they don't have enough customers buying from them on a regular basis. Either they're not attracting enough new customers, or they're letting their existing customers slip away.

Now think about the people we're talking about here… they're entrepreneurs and business leaders; these are people who are doers, people who make things happen. So it's highly unlikely their failure is because they don't try. It's almost always because they don't have the expertise and experience to create effective customer generating and customer retention strategies… or business development marketing strategies.

In this program I'm going to show you three secrets to achieving unbelievable and exponential growth for your business, even during a slow economy or recession. And these three simple concepts aren't that difficult to understand or implement in any business.

So if you're ready, if your mind is open to the incredible possibilities, let's get started.

USP / Differentiation

The first key to achieving incredible, exponential growth is to be unique in an advantageous way to your prospects and customers, and to be able to communicate that uniqueness effectively and consistently to your target market.

You must create a marketing message that is clear, compelling and quantifiable. Then you must articulate and communicate that message to your market every chance you get.

This is so incredibly important because it is the foundation of all your marketing and sales efforts, and your entire business for that matter. Ultimately, it's the reason why your prospects should do business with you over all your competition.

There are many names for this strategy, such as creating a Unique Selling Proposition, or a Unique Competitive Advantage. For the purpose of this program we're going to keep it simple and use the most common term, which is Unique Selling Proposition, or USP. This is the term that advertising guru Rosser Reeves created and first wrote about in the 1950's and 60's, so I'll use his term and give him the credit.

Your USP is what separates you from all your competition, both locally and industry wide… it is what makes you unique.

Think about it… Today's consumers have more choices available to them than at any other time in history. So now, more than ever, you need to be different and able to give your market a valid reason why they should do business with you over all of their other options… over all of your competitors.

Have you ever noticed that the most successful businesses in an industry or profession aren't always the best, but they are almost always considered unique in some way that's important to their market.

There are so many "me too" businesses that rarely survive because they don't have any unique attributes to help them establish value in the minds of their prospects. So they cut prices and end up in price wars, because that's the only marketing weapon they have with which to compete. And unless you have a significant cost advantage over all of your competitors, it's only a matter of time until you lose this battle.

Let's imagine that I'm a potential customer for your business. Why should I do business with you instead of any and all other options available to me?

What makes you so special, different, or unique? Why should I spend my money with you, rather than with your competitors? What can I get from you that I can't get from anyone else that sells the same product or service, or at least a reasonable substitute?

Because creating and using your USP is such an important component of growing your business, and because very few business owners and managers really take this concept to heart, I want you to perform a little test… I promise it will be a great learning experience for you.

Ask ten business owners, or professionals, managers, entrepreneurs, or sales people why you should do business with them and not their competitors, and you'll most likely get the same generic answers over and over again..

Some of these generic answers include: "we offer the highest quality products or services", or "we offer the best customer service", or maybe "we have the lowest prices around."

After you hear their answer, ask yourself this question: what did you really learn from that kind of statement? Does their answer really inspire you to purchase from them? Or is their answer another "me-too", boring and forgetful statement that you've heard a million times before?

So if you're in business, or if you're in any way responsible for attracting new customers to your business, then it's an absolute imperative that you have a clear and compelling answer to the question of why someone should do business with you and not your competition. If you don't, then I promise you that you're underperforming.

Competition today is so fierce, products and services are so similar, and prices are so cutthroat… it's almost impossible in any industry or profession to maintain a competitive advantage for very long because of the product or service you offer, or the price you charge.

The simple truth is that if you can't give your prospects and customers a clear and compelling reason to buy from you, they you should never expect your business to be any better than your competitors… and you'll just be another "me-too" business in the eyes of your customers and market.

That's why you must have something to offer your customers and clients that your competition doesn't, and preferably something they can't offer. And whatever that something is, you need to identify it, quantify it, and articulate it in a compelling way in all of your marketing efforts.

And that something is what your USP is. It's your defining statement of what makes your business stand out and unique in a competitive marketplace of "me-too" businesses. It's what will differentiate you from your competition, and it will give you an unmatched competitive advantage.

Now this is not a new concept, but most businesses, including your competitors, don't have a clue how to do it properly. Like I said earlier, ask 10 business owners, managers or sales people why you should buy from them and not their competition. I doubt you hear even one that has a unique, compelling answer.

And if you asked 100, I bet you wouldn't find more than 1 or 2 who had an answer so strong that it stopped you in your tracks and made you interested in their products or services.

Now let me give you a few examples of some of the all-time great USPs:

- The most famous example is probably Domino's Pizza: Fresh, hot pizza delivered to your door in 30 minutes or less, guaranteed. That USP guaranteeing delivery took Domino's Pizza from a start up to a 4 billion dollar company in just a few years.

- And there's the "confidence inspiring" FedEx USP – When it absolutely, positively has to be there over night.

- Another great one is M&M's – melts in your mouth, not in your hands.

- And Lens Crafter – helping people see better one hour at a time.

- And one that was used a few years back – You won't find airbags as standard equipment in those Japanese cars, only in Chryslers.

Do you see how those USPs clearly position those businesses as being different from their competition? If a buyer wanted the benefits they promise, they're the one who provides them. And that's a competitive advantage you need to have in your business.

Coming up with your USP doesn't have to be difficult, but it does have to be considered valuable by your target market. Remember, it's not what you think that counts, it's what your prospects and customers think… and since they're the ones with the money, it's their vote that counts.

Because this component of positioning your business is such a crucial part of your marketing program, TriFecta Marketing makes sure we get it right for our customers. I've developed a comprehensive 10-step process to help you create a USP that will separate you from all your competitors and make every other aspect of your sales and marketing stronger.

And once your USP has been created, I help you integrate it into everything you do. Remember, this is one of the most powerful marketing weapons you will ever have, so it's crucial to get it right and then include it in all of your marketing and business operations. And why shouldn't you? It's a statement that sums up what your entire business is about.

Understanding Business Growth

Now let's talk about the second key to achieving exponential growth for your business, even in a slow economy, and that is to understand how your business actually grows, and leverage this knowledge to your advantage.

When you get down to it, everything you do to grow your business can be classified under three primary categories, and if you learn how to leverage this properly, you can achieve unbelievable results.

This concept is so powerful, and proper implementation of this model makes achieving growth so much easier, that I named my company after it. I call it the TriFecta Exponential Growth Model, and with it your competition won't stand a chance. Because not only does your competition not understand this how this model works, most have never heard or thought about it, much less put it to work for their advantage.

Increasing New Customers

The first of the three categories of growing your business, and the first part of the TriFecta Exponential Growth Model, is to increase your number of customers. Pretty simple... When more people buy from you, you make more money.

It's in this one single growth area that most business owners, including your competition, and probably you, too, focus most of their time, efforts, and marketing dollars.

But if you've been in business any length of time, you probably realize that getting new customers isn't always the easiest or most profitable thing you can do, and it's almost always the most expensive component of your marketing.

Let's take a look at this category of business growth at deeper level. Every business, association or professional practice needs new customers and clients; they wouldn't survive without them. But few businesses really understand what has to happen to get new customers to purchase from them.

You see, there are several marketing functions involved in the process of producing new customers, and they may differ from business to business. The most common functions include lead generation, prospect education, prospect conversion (or closing customers), and generating referrals.

All of these processes are important, but for many small and mid-size businesses, lead generation is the only purpose of their marketing. I hope this is not the case for you. If it is, I hope that after hearing this audio presentation that you do something to remedy that problem.

What is the typical sequence of events that must take place in your business for you to create a new customer? You may find an additional step in your Customer Generation Process, and that's not a problem. The important thing to understand is that you must identify these steps and lead your prospects through the entire process. Customer Generation and lead generation are not the same.

So many businesses never reach their potential because prospects and customers fall through the holes in their marketing process. Don't let this happen to you.

Increasing Average Transaction Value

Getting new customers is important to every business, but there are two more primary methods of business growth you need to understand, and both of these methods are more profitable, more effective, and give you greater potential for leverage than increasing new customers.

Method number two for growing your business, and the second part of the TriFecta Exponential Growth Model, is to increase your customer's average transaction value, or to get your customers to spend more money every time they buy from you. This is one of the quickest and easiest methods you will find to increase your profits.

I find it amazing how many business owners have expensive plans in place to generate new customers, but very few have paid much attention to the highly profitable step of increasing the size of the average order.

Let me give you an example to show you how easy it is… and how profitable it can be, so you'll see why it's such a powerful concept.

Let's take the fast food restaurant industry as an example. They have completely embraced this concept and are masters of upselling and cross-selling techniques.

Think about the last time you went through a fast food drive through… You drive up, place your order, and a voice comes back over the speaker and asks if you want fries or a hot apple pie with your order. This is an example of a cross-sell, or selling an additional product along with the original purchase.

Or maybe they suggest you super size your order. This is an example of an upsell, or increasing the size of the initial order.

In either case, if you take them up on one of their suggestions, what they have done is substantially increase their profits. They have increased their sale and had no customer acquisition or marketing costs associated with it.

You see, the owners and managers of the fast food restaurants understand that a certain percentage of their customer will say yes, and the only reason they say yes is because a suggestion was made to them. It's a numbers game, and those numbers become predictable increases in profits every single day.

But cross-selling and up-selling aren't the only techniques these savvy marketers use to increase the average customer transaction value. They are also experts at a technique called packaging, or bundling. This is when they combine a drink and fries, or maybe a cookie or toy with the order and call it a combo or a happy meal.

You benefit because you pay less for the package than those items purchased separately would cost, but the total dollar amount you spend is higher. And again, since there were no marketing costs involved, the only cost being for the items themselves, it's pure profits that go straight to the bottom line.

Now what about you? You may not be in the fast food business, but the principles apply to just about everyone. Ask yourself this question: what additional products or services do you have that would naturally compliment what your customers are initially buying from you?

Can you suggest your customers upgrade to a better model? Maybe you can offer them a larger quantity or a more comprehensive or frequent application? Can you find ways to bundle or package items together to give your customers more benefits or added value while at the same time increasing your unit of sale?

If you want to be effective at this, it's important to understand what is actually happening. You see, you have an obligation to your customers and clients to make sure they get the most value, benefit, and enjoyment from the products and services they purchase from you. And if you have additional products and services that can enhance their value, then it's your obligation to do everything reasonable and ethical to make sure they at least have the option of taking advantage of that added value.

Again, when you're presenting upsells, cross-sells, and packaged offers, it's a numbers game. Some will take advantage of your offer and some won't, but at least you will have given them the opportunity to receive additional value. You haven't made the decision for them; you've given them a choice to decide for themselves.

And if you are sincerely trying to add value, they won't see you as being pushy; they will see you as trying to help them get more value for their purchase. And this is important, since customers aren't really purchasing products and services from you, they are buying solutions and benefits.

Can you see how much common sense this makes? But as I said before, it's surprising how few businesses actually take advantage of these three simple business growth techniques.

There are a dozen different methods that I use to increase the average transaction value for my clients, upselling, cross-selling and packaging are only a few of them. And if you don't do anything other than find a way to implement these three techniques in your business, you will blast your profits completely through the roof.

Now if you don't think this is possible, I've personally done it with clients ranging from insurance and investment companies, to seminar companies, computer resellers and software companies, restaurants, medical and legal practices, fitness chains, and charitable organizations. In fact, it's worked in every company I've tried to implement this strategy with, and it can work for you, too.

You're increasing sales without increasing marketing expenses, and you can add an additional 20, 30, or 40% or more to your profits by doing it properly. In fact, there are several companies that I know of that have more than doubled their profits per transaction by implementing these programs. But the real question is what can you do?

Increasing Purchase Frequency

Now let's move on to the third method of growing your business, and the third component of the TriFecta Exponential Growth Model, and that's to increase your customer purchase frequency, or get your customers to buy from you more often.

Think about this: the longer your customers go between purchases from you, the greater chance they have of leaving and buying from your competition. You've heard the saying "out of sight, out of mind", well that couldn't be more true than it is in business.

In fact, for every month that your customers don't have meaningful contact with your business, you lose about 10% of your top of mind awareness. That means that in less than a year you can be completely forgotten, and you cannot allow this to happen.

You need to have a plan to constantly stay in front of your customers with information they will care about, information they will value. This can range from sales and special promotion, to announcements and explanations of new products and services, to other offers and information that might benefit them. The key is to be fun and to lead them to believe that they would be foolish to do business with anyone else other than you.

Now let's think about this concept for your business? What could you do to endear your customers to you, to lock them into doing business with you and keep them away from your competition, and get them coming back more often? What are you doing? Do you have an educational newsletter? Do you send personal letters? Do you use email? Do you have a website that keeps them abreast of what's new?

Here's another important question you need to know the answer to: How long, on average, do the customers who buy from you remain your customers? How long do they continue to do business with you before they move on?

Are they one-time buyers, or do they stay with you for a year, two years, five years, or ten years? And what are you doing in your business right now to make sure that your customers continue to do business with you, and not move on to your competitors?

Your marketing plan needs to contain strategic systems to not only keep your customers coming back, but to keep them coming back forever. If it doesn't, you are losing more customers each year to your competition than you have to.

I want you to think about this for a moment, and this is very important...

Right now your competition is making plans and taking steps to steal your customers away from you. So the question you must ask yourself is this: What are you doing about it? What systems do you currently have in place to keep your customers from defecting to your competitors?

What are you doing to make your customers thrilled to do business with you? Notice I didn't say satisfied, because there's a huge difference between being thrilled and satisfied. Last year more than 200 million Americans stopped doing business with companies they were satisfied with, and 60% of so called satisfied customers switch companies or brands on a regular basis.

You can't afford to not thrill your customers or to work to build trust in you and your business. But unfortunately, most business owners don't understand this.

As I mentioned earlier, the marketing dollars and efforts of most businesses are directed at getting new customers or the first sale… or what's called the front end. They spend a disproportionate amount of time looking for new customers when the real gold mine is found in the back end, or continuing sales from repeat customers.

You may not like hearing this, but if you're spending money on marketing or advertising to bring in new customers, but you're not proactively working to get those customers purchasing from you again and again, then you're flushing that advertising investment down the toilet.

Now in order for you to market to your past and current customers, you will need to have a means of contacting them. I know this sounds simplistic, but the vast majority of small business owners either don't have a customer and prospect database, or don't communicate with their database on a regular basis.

One of the most important things you will ever do in your business is capture customer information at the point of sale. For some businesses this information is captured automatically in the sales process, but for others businesses you will need to ask for it.

And once you have this information about your customers, you need to use it. Here's why…

It cost 5 to 8 times more to market to get a new customer to purchase from you, than it does to get a repeat customer to purchase from you again.

Even though the new customer may generate the same amount of income, the profits are substantially lower because your customer acquisition costs are 5 to 8 times higher.

What percentage of your marketing efforts and dollars are directed at getting your existing customers to purchase from you more often?

For most business, optimizing this strategy alone can increase their bottom line profits by 20% - 50%.

I was hired by an already very successful restaurant group that owned seven restaurants in a large city that ranged from fine dining to pubs. The goal was simple: help them make more money.

Because of the nature of my agreement with this group, I can't go into many specifics, but I can say that we were effective at implementing three different programs to increase customer purchase frequency at seven different restaurants. On average we were able to increase profits by about $15,000 per restaurant per month. That's an average of $180,000 of new profits per year, per restaurant, or a total of $1.26 million combined new profits.

What's even more important is that the cost to create, implement and maintain the entire program is less than $20,000 per year. A less than $20,000 a year investment produces a return of over $1.2 million dollars per year. Now that's not a bad ROI.

Now think about how this whole concept relates to your business. What is it that you can do, specifically, to get your customers to purchase from you more often, and to extend your customers buying lifetime?

With TriFecta Marketing, I utilize over two dozen different strategies that create an almost magnetic effect of keeping your customers returning time and time again, that help you hang on to them for longer, that keeps them insulated from, and locked out of your competition.

Creating a Business Growth Plan

So there you go… the three methods of growing your business, and the three components of the TriFecta Exponential Growth Model: increasing your number of customers, increasing the average transaction size, and increasing customer purchase frequency.

We're going to come back to this in a minute, but for now I want to jump to the third key in creating exponential growth for your business, even in a slow economy… And that key is to create and implement a comprehensive business development marketing plan based on the information I've covered in this audio presentation.

I'm going to be very honest with you: if you want your business to be successful, you have to make getting and keeping customers your number one priority. And getting and keeping customers is the purpose of marketing.

Let me put that a different way: the principle objective of your business is marketing your business, because if you don't have any customers, you don't have a business.

Huge leaps in business success come from only one place: sales and marketing. Nobody gets rich as a technician or managing employees, yet so many entrepreneurs and business owners let such things suck up their time, spending it on everything but sales and marketing.

The sooner you understand this, the sooner you will create your own business breakthrough: the place for you to direct your time, energy, common sense and money is in marketing.

There's an old advertising saying that goes like this: "any fool can make soap, but it takes a clever man to sell it." You see, even if it's the best soap on the planet, it won't matter if no one buys it.

I'm sure you don't want to think of your business as the maker of just another piece of soap, but that's exactly what it is. There's a thousand other people out there that do what you do.

You may be an accounting wizard, or maybe you are an awesome manufacturer of mousetraps or widgets... but so are 100 others whose ad sits right next to yours in the yellow pages and other media.

I want to share with you one of my favorite business quotes by one of the most important business minds in history. This is what Peter Drucker had to say about marketing: *"Because its purpose is to create a customer, a business has just two functions: marketing and innovation.*

Marketing and innovation produce results, everything else is a cost."

That's pretty powerful. Marketing is the most important investment in your business, because the purpose of your business is to create a customer.

Now there's one more quote that I want to share with you by the person considered to be the world's foremost expert on small business, and that's Michael Gerber. In Gerber's book titled the E-Myth, he states that "most entrepreneurs fail because they spend too much time working in their business, and not enough time working on their business."

And marketing is the tool you use to work on your business.

Suppose you were really able to internalize this critical principle. Suppose you truly came to believe that the most important function in your business is the marketing of your products and services. What would you do differently? Would you allocate and prioritize your time differently? Would you change the amount of money that you invest to grow your business?

Believe it or not, most small businesses I've been exposed to over the years don't have a marketing plan. But over and over again, studies show that small businesses that have a marketing plan consistently outperform competitors who don't have marketing plans by an average of 30%.

But let's give entrepreneurs and small businesses a break. The most common reason that they don't have marketing plans is very simple: most entrepreneurs are doers, rather than planners. And in reality, being a doer is perhaps the ultimate mark of a successful person. It's what makes entrepreneurs a rare breed. Rather than thinking or wishing, they get out there and make something happen.

But so many small business owners get into trouble by not only doing the wrong marketing activities, but doing them incorrectly. Of course, what you want to do is choose the right marketing activities and do them the right way… and this starts with a marketing plan.

Now you don't have to kill a tree to produce an effective marketing plan that will guide and propel your business far ahead of where it is now. In fact, you can create a successful marketing plan for your small business in a very short time.

The key is having an effective marketing strategy and creating a powerful, comprehensive business development marketing plan.

Let's turn our focus to a couple of key words I'm using to describe a marketing plan…

First of all, I didn't say you just needed a marketing plan, I said "business development marketing plan." The purpose of a business development marketing plan is simply to develop your business, or grow your business. And this is achieved by increasing sales, increasing profits, and increasing market share. That's what we focus on with a business development marketing plan.

Second, I use the word "comprehensive." What I mean by a "comprehensive marketing plan" is that it is focused on achieving exponential growth, or growing the business in all three methods.

Exponential Growth Examples

OK , so what exactly is exponential growth and how is it different from typical business growth. That's a good question and its most easily answered by giving you an example based on the information we've already covered.

We're going to create a fictitious business using some simple numbers for this demonstration. If you would like to follow along using numbers from your business, then grab yourself a pen, paper and a calculator... and get ready to have a little fun.

Let's say you have a business in which you have 1000 customers, that spend an average of $100 per purchase, and they buy from you an average of 10 times per year. What you end up with is a $1,000,000 per year in business.

Now let's say that you were able to improve each of the three primary growth areas by 10%, which is a conservative number that is usually easy to achieve.

You would then have 1100 customers, spending $110 per transaction, 11 times each year, for a business doing $1,331,000 per year. That's a total growth of your business by 33.1%.

10% growth in customers, multiplied by 10% growth in average transaction value, multiplied by 10% growth in purchase frequency doesn't equal 30% growth. It totals 33.1% growth.

Let's say you were able to make 20% improvements in each of the three growth areas. 20% + 20% +20 doesn't equal 60%, it equals an incredible 72.8%. Can you see the synergistic effect that's going on here? The total growth of the business is much greater than the sum of each of the growth areas. This is exponential growth.

Again, I'm using 10% and 20% growth because they're nice round numbers that are easy to work with. Let's look at another example, but this time let's mix the numbers up a bit.

Let's say that we were able to increase the number of customers by 19%, from 1000 to 1190 total customers. And let's also say we were only able to increase purchase frequency by 7%, from an average of 10 purchases to 10.7 purchases per year. Finally, let's say we increased the average transaction value by 23%, from $100 to $123 per transaction.

Our new sales totals are $1,566,159, or a TrFecta Exponential Growth rate of 56.6%... and with a comprehensive business development marketing program, this is very realistic. In fact, it can actually get even better when you create what I call a TriFecta Marketing Machine.

Up to this point I've discussed the three categories of business growth that comprise the TriFecta Exponential Growth Model. They are increasing the total number of customers, increasing the average transaction value, and increasing customer purchase frequency. All business growth falls under these three categories.

But what I haven't told you about are the sub-categories of the TriFecta Growth Model. Just like the three categories of business growth, these sub-categories can be improved and optimized to make an even more significant impact on your bottom line.

These sub-categories include increasing the number of referrals you receive, increasing your conversion (or closing rates), improving your lead generation effectiveness, reactivating your inactive customers, and reducing customer attrition, which is the number of customers you lose every year.

These are all areas of focus in a comprehensive business development marketing plan, and when you put them all together you can achieve business growth that you probably never thought was possible, and you create what I call a TriFecta Marketing Machine.

Let's create one more example, this time factoring in all the components of business growth. To do this we'll use our same fictitious business and baseline of making small, 10% improvements in each of the key areas.

But before I give you the results, let me share with you the realistic numbers I used in this calculation:

- For lead generation, I'm using 100 leads generated monthly.

- For prospect conversion, I'm using a 10% closing ratio.

- This equates to 10 new customers each month.

- For customer attrition, or the percentage of customers a business loses each year, I chose a very conservative number that works across almost all industries, and that is 20%.

- For customer reactivation, I'm assuming that there are three years of inactive customers in the database. One-thousand customers annually, multiplied by the 20% you lose each year to attrition, multiplied by 3 years, equals a total of 600 inactive customers.

The results... our $1million dollar a year business doubles into a $2million dollar a year TriFecta Marketing Machine. Again, we're only making small, 10% improvements in key areas, and when you have this logical and systematic approach, doubling your business doesn't seem so impossible.

The concept of Exponential Growth is incredible, and it's not just theory. The truth is that smart marketers, entrepreneurs and business leaders have been using these principles for years, and this type of growth is attainable for almost any established small or mid-sized business. The key is that you must approach it from an intelligent and comprehensive business development marketing perspective.

If you're at all like most business owners, managers, or entrepreneurs, you're thinking about how the TriFecta Exponential Growth Model applies to your specific business and your specific situation. And that's good… it's the first step in creating your own TriFecta Marketing Machine.

Let me assure you, this growth strategy is based on solid business principles, and I've never had anyone disagree with this… from CPA's to CEO's and CFO's of Fortune 1000 and Inc 500 businesses. Business principles are business principles, the only difference is in how you apply them in each specific business.

Example: Exponential Growth

Creating a implementing a comprehensive business development marketing plan can produce tremendous results in the growth of your business. Let me give you a couple of client examples that demonstrate that point.

I was hired by a young consulting practice specializing in services to the telecom industry. They were ready for growth but needed to create a sales and marketing breakthrough to realize their goals.

The first goal we had was to increase their customer base. To accomplish this we created a strong Unique Selling Proposition and optimized the lead generation programs and customer generation processes that they were already using.

Our second goal was to increase average transaction values. This was achieved by creating several different service packages and by designing an effective system to upsell and cross-sell their prospects and customers to these higher value, higher priced programs.

With these programs we were able to increase annual sales from just over $400,000 per year, to $2.2 million in only 9 months.

Now I'm not going to tell you these are typical results… in many different ways a business has to be ready for this type of rapid growth. But TTS was ready, and our results were incredible.

Example: The Wellness Center

Another example is of an established, multi-doctor, holistic medical clinic I worked with that provided chiropractic, massage therapy, reflexology, and herbal medicine services.

Having been operational for over 15 years, their growth had stagnated in the last couple of years. We created a comprehensive business development marketing program based on education, client communication, cross selling and packaging techniques, and adding several new streams of new clients. The results – we were able to almost double the total yearly revenues of The Wellness Center in only one year.

Now how difficult would it be to achieve this kind of growth in your business? Could you realistically increase each of the primary growth areas by 10%? What about 20%? The honest answer is I don't know. But that doesn't really matter.

The truth is that some areas may not apply to your situation... but it's definitely worth exploring.

Marketing in a Slow Economy

Now I want to get to the last topic I promised to cover in this audio program, and that's about marketing your business in a slow economy or a recession.

Now there's a reason I saved this part for last, and that's because all the strategies and concepts that I've covered up to this point are actually more applicable and important to you during a recessive economy, and in many ways they are more powerful and advantageous as well.

Think about it this way, consumers don't go away during a recession, they just become more conservative. They don't stop spending money, but they do scrutinize their purchases more carefully to make certain they are getting the best value.

And for well positioned companies, this represents an incredible opportunity to inexpensively capture market share and leap ahead of your competition.

Case Studies

Let's take a look at the results some very revealing studies have proven.

A study conducted by Cathers Publishing and SPI, between 1982 to 2007, showed that focused marketing during a recession produces greater gains in market share than during strong times, while decreases in marketing produces greater loss in market share.

Another study conducted by McGraw-Hill following the 1981-82 recession, evaluated the performance of 600 business to business firms. It found that those companies who maintained or increased marketing during the recession grew sales 275% between the years 1980-85. Sales of firms that cut marketing averaged only 19% growth during the same time period.

If you've studied business success and business development marketing, you will find dozens of amazing success stories by many of the largest, most accomplished corporations in the world... and over a stretch of many different economic recessions.

Recession Success Stories

Let me give you a few examples that you may recognize:

- Back in 1919, in the middle of the Post WWI Recession, Schlitz Beer went from 15th position in their industry to first... all within 6 months.

- During the Great Depression, Kellogg stole the market from Post and Sears took the market from Wards.

- During the recession of 1990-91, Taco Bell and Pizza Hut had their greatest growth periods, and Intel captured the market with their brilliant "Intel Inside" marketing campaign.

Think about the strongest brands and great marketing machines of the world… Do you think that Coke, Nike, Wal-Mart, and McDonalds stop marketing during a recession or slow economy? No, they wouldn't even consider it. In fact, they have a history of using these periods as an opportunity to capture more market share from their competitors.

Now all these examples are of huge corporations, not small and mid-size businesses. But the reality is that it is much easier for smaller, more flexible business to take advantage of recessive economic conditions than it is for companies operating internationally at the highest levels, with the most sophisticated competitors.

Recession Marketing Tips

Smart, business development marketing can become your business' best friend during a slow economy, but how do you do it? What should you -- the small or mid-size business owner, manager or sales professional -- do to be a more effective marketer and to capture market share?

USP

At the beginning of this presentation we reviewed the USP, or the Unique Selling Proposition. It's the reason why your market chooses your business, products and services over all other options available to them, including all of your competitors.

Having a strong USP that differentiates and substantiates your business in your marketplace is the first key to not only surviving a recessive economy, but it allows you to continue growing when all your competitors are hunkering down and just trying to survive.

During a recession, more so than in any other time, you can't be seen as just a "me-too" business. You have to be different... you have to be more advantageous to your customers and market than all of your competitors. And if you're not different or more advantageous, you have to figure out a way that you can be.

Now once you've developed a strong Unique Selling Proposition that gives your market a compelling reason why they should do business with you over all your competitors, you need to create a plan to survive and thrive, and you need to be smarter with your marketing dollars.

Notice that I said you need to be smarter with your market dollars, I didn't say you needed to cut your marketing budget.

Most small and mid-size business owners and managers make the dangerous mistake of cutting their marketing budget. But why would you cut the one function in your business that is an investment in your success and growth, and that can increase your sales and profits?

Recession Marketing Plan

It's time to get smart with your marketing, and to do this you need an intelligent marketing plan to guide and propel you through the slow economy. Now, we just covered the benefits of the marketing plan, but I want you to understand that it's even more important to have one during a recession.

You see, you always want to maintain as much control over your business and your future as possible. And the process of creating a well-thought-out marketing plan to not only guide you through a tough economy, but position you above and beyond your competition, is very empowering.

The marketing plan that you create to succeed during a slow economy needs to embrace the formula for achieving exponential growth, and for established businesses, you need to focus more of your efforts on your customer database.

Focus on Existing Customers

For the average business, for almost any given period of time, only 15% of their customers are first time buyers. That means 85% are repeat customers.

And since it cost 5 to 8 times more to find new customers than to retain current ones, you can spend a lot less money to produce the same results if you focus on marketing to your existing customers.

For almost any business the customer database is the most important asset they have, and huge opportunities exists for those that use it properly. Because a well maintained and effectively utilized database can increase customer purchase frequency, improve customer loyalty, drive referral business, and reduce customer attrition.

So creating, maintaining, and effectively utilizing your customer database needs to become one of your highest priorities.

Advertising Tips

Just a moment ago I said that during a recession businesses need to be more prudent and wise with their marketing dollars. On that topic, I want to cover one last subject as it pertains to marketing during recessive periods, and that's advertising.

There are several reasons I want to touch on this subject. First, it's one of the most common forms of marketing, and there's a good chance that many of the small and mid-size business owners, managers, and marketers that are listening to this program are already advertising.

Second, advertising can be a wonderful investment in building your business, or it can be a huge waste of money. Unfortunately for most businesses, it's a waste of money.

OK, so here's your first tip about advertising during a recession: If you do any advertising to acquire new customers and leads, use only direct response advertising, not institutional or image advertising.

One of the most misunderstood concepts in marketing is that the purpose of an advertisement is to keep a company or business' name in front of their prospects... so that when they're ready to buy, they'll contact you.

Now there may be some validity to this, but as a small or mid-size business owner or executive, the most important reason for advertising in any media, is to get your intended audience to respond to an offer you're making, or to drive sales to your business.

Institutional or image advertising, is the type of advertising most businesses use, but it serves little practical purpose to small businesses. It's all about getting your name out to your market and building awareness, and that is a problem.

You see, there's no way to track the results on these image advertisements, therefore you won't really know if they're effective or not. You won't know how much new business was created, and you won't know what the return is for your marketing investment.

For any small or mid-size business or professional practice, the purpose of your advertising should be to generate leads and sales. Getting your name out to your market is secondary.

You see, any advertisement, regardless if it's in print, on the air, a direct mail letter or postcard, anything… no matter what form your advertisement takes, you need to consider it as salesmanship in that particular media or form.

I'm going to give you an easy way to understand this point…

Imagine this: would you send out a salesperson to visit a prospect and have them say "Hi, I'm with ABC Widget Company. I just wanted you to know that we're here and to remember us if you ever need widgets."

Not a very strong sales pitch, is it? There was no offer, and there was no strong and compelling reason to buy.

But that's exactly what image advertising does. It doesn't motivate your prospects to take action now, and that's not a good recipe for building your business.

If you want your advertising to be effective, it should include a compelling offer that stimulates an immediate response from your audience. Not only that, it must be accountable, measureable and trackable. With direct response advertising, you will be able to measure the effectiveness of your ad by the number of people that respond to your offer. Again, you can't do that with Image advertising.

Many small business owners and marketers make the mistake of trying to copy the marketing of larger, brand name businesses, and unfortunately end up wasting a lot of money and seeing very little results from their efforts. And often this leads them to thinking that advertising, or marketing in general, just doesn't work for them.

But advertising does work, and it can work incredibly well if you do it properly. Think about this for a second...

If you think that advertising doesn't work, there are 30 mountains in Colorado that are higher than Pike's Peak. Can you name one of them?

I doubt I've ever seen a business that couldn't make advertising work for them if they approached it properly. But because so many business owners, executives and marketers don't know how to create advertising that produces real results, they give up on it and miss out on this incredible business building workhorse.

You see, it's foolish for a small or mid-size business to try to copy the advertising of big, brand-name companies. First of all, you don't have the same agenda with your advertising as these big corporations do. Often they are concerned with looking good to their stockholders and board of directors, look good to Wall Street, build brand awareness, and even winning awards for their advertising.

If the purpose of your advertising is to sell something, you need to forget about image advertising and focus on direct response. If you're going to emulate someone else, emulate a successful business that has the same goals you have… to sell products and services.

For now I just want you to understand that you should never run an ad just to build awareness or get your name out. You should only run direct response ads, especially during a recession, that you can track, measure and that will produce leads and sales for you immediately.

Advertising Example

There have been dozens of occasions when I've been asked to re-work advertisements that run in various media that range from local and trade publications, to infomercials, to radio and web based advertising.

Now because there was no effective way to measure the results of most of the advertisements, we often didn't have a baseline to gauge improvements. However, on those we could compare results, I've seen improvements in response from a low end of 100%, to an average of about 300%, and I've even seen measureable increases in response of over 2000%... all by just using proper direct response techniques in your advertising.

Role of Creative

The second topic I want to cover regarding advertising is to understand the role of "creative" in advertising.

When it comes to producing actual results of increased sales, very few successful advertisements come from brand new, creative ideas. Instead, most successful advertisements are alterations or combinations of already proven winners, usually with only a small "twist" of originality.

So many so called marketing and advertising "experts" try to sell you on creative, new ideas. There's a lot of reasons why they do this... they have fun with it, they may be able to win awards for it, and they can bill you for it.

Now I'm not saying that their creative ideas don't work, but understand that when you do something new and unproven, then you're gambling. I don't know about you, but as a small business owner I would prefer to have something that's proven to work time and time again.

If someone tries to sell you on the concept of creating an ad that is unique and creative, ask f you can pay them based on the results the ad produces for you. I doubt you find anyone who will take you up on that offer.

Negotiation Tips

The third recession advertising tip I have for you is to negotiate hard with media reps for lower rates. There's a couple of ways you can do this that work pretty well during a recession.

First, you can ask for remnant space, or the space that remains unsold when the advertising deadline approaches. You see, it's very likely that many of their advertisers are cutting their advertising budgets because of the slowing economy.

Often the media will sell the unsold, or remnant space at a substantial discount just to get something for it. Otherwise they would be forced to include "filler" ads, editorial or additional stories in that space. It's not like they will leave that space blank.

I'll be honest with you, you're probably not going to get a media rep or their manager to agree to this approach in the beginning. But if you're persistent when they call on you, you may just get yourself a great deal.

Another option is to ask for volume discounts. Almost all media offer them, and they can be significant. However, I wouldn't suggest entering a long-term commitment with any media until you've tested it, it has proven itself to work for you, and you can predict what kind of return on your advertising investment you will receive.

Remember, you're using direct response advertising techniques, and you will be able to measure and track the results.

And speaking of results, you must always closely monitor and measure the results of your marketing efforts. If you don't, you have no real basis of making intelligent marketing decisions, and you won't know if it makes good business sense to continue running, or cancel an ad or marketing program.

If it works, keep doing it. If it doesn't, dump it and find something that does work to invest your marketing budget into.

So those are a few recession marketing tips for you. Now when you consider that almost all of your competitors will be tightening their purse strings and cutting their marketing, do you see the opportunity? Stealing market share and customers from your competition is a bargain during a recession, and will pay great dividends in long term profitability for your company.

Conclusion

When put to work for you, the ideas and strategies covered in this audio program have the potential of turning your business into a dominant force in your market and virtually eliminating your competition. These ideas and strategies will work for you and your business just like they've worked for thousands of other businesses in hundreds of different industries and professions. But they can't work by themselves... they only work if you take action.

You see, right now your business is on trial. Your customers and prospects are the jury, your business is the defendant, and as a leader in your business, you're the attorney. Every time a decision is made regarding the potential purchase of the products and services you sell, your customers and prospects, the jury, issue a ruling.

Here's a question for you: how will your customers and prospects rule today? Will they hand down the death sentence by giving their business to your competitors? Will they sentence you to business imprisonment or probation, still alive, but barely surviving?

Or have you presented them with enough evidence for your business to go free and continue growing, thriving and serving the marketplace with improved products, better services, and more benefits for your customers and clients.

Now if you ask most people, they will tell you that the fate of your business rests in the hands of the jury, your prospects and customers. That they're the ones will allow you to remain in business or get the death penalty.

To some extent this is true, but they base their verdict, they base their decision on the evidence that's been presented to them... The evidence that you, as the attorney, or as the owner or manager of the business have given them.

So how about that evidence? What is the depth and the quality of the evidence you've presented? Have you given them so much evidence as to why they should buy the products and services you offer, that they really don't have any other choice?

Have you presented facts, figures and data, and have you included testimony from expert witnesses, or your satisfied customers. Have you lead them to the undeniable conclusion that they would be fools to do business with anyone else but you?

You see, it's up to you to present a convincing argument to your jury. It's up to you to prove beyond a reasonable doubt why they should do business with you and not even consider your competition.

Right now, right this very minute, your competition is making plans and taking steps to take your customers away from you; to steal your market share and prevent you from getting any new customers. So what are you going to do to keep this from happening?

This can be a terrifying thought for any business owner, leader or entrepreneur, that's not trained and experienced in getting maximum response from your efforts in business development marketing.

Statistics show that out of 1,000,000 new businesses that will start up this year, over 40% will fail before the year is up, and 80% will never see their 5th anniversary. And if that's not bad enough, 80% of those remaining won't make it another 5 years.

But it doesn't have to be that way. There are things you can do, that any person can do to not only survive in business, but to grow and prosper... And we've only talked about a few of those things in our time together.

But let me just say that the ideas and strategies that I've shared with you, and that I go into great detail in creating and implementing with my clients, they work.

They have the potential of putting thousands of dollars in your pocket. I've seen businesses that were struggling to make ends meet apply business development marketing strategies, and in a very short time turn their businesses completely around. And because they're based on sound business development principles and smart marketing practices, they will work for you, too.

On a base level your business is really no different than any other business in any other industry or profession. Business development principles are the same; it's only how they're applied that is different.

You want the same things that every other business owner wants: increased sales, profits and market share. And your customers want the same thing that every customer of every market wants: the best value for the money they spend, and they want to feel they are appreciated. And those two areas are exactly what TriFecta Marketing addresses.

Now, if you rely on a sales team to generate your customers, then business development marketing can be a great tool to make your team more efficient and effective. I've used business development marketing to help an established company in a commoditized industry increase the entire team's average closing ratio by 400%. On top of that, I have a start-up client that I assisted in product development, strategy and messaging, who is closing over 80% of their sales.

So if you want to increases sales, profits or market share, it's business development marketing that you should turn to.

Now there's something important that I have to tell you. My business development programs are not for everyone. I'm only interested in working with serious people who have aggressive business goals. They must be open minded, ready to move forward, and dedicated to growing their businesses.

They need to want to control their business future; they must want to create multiple streams of new customers; and they must want to position their businesses as not only the logical choice for their market, but as the only intelligent choice.

You see, I can only work with a certain number of clients at one time, and my time is too valuable to work with people that are half hearted or not ready to make the necessary commitment. And it's not fair to those who are ready, who are willing, who are motivated… to give the time they want to those with only a luke-warm commitment.

I have an obligation to those I do business with to see that they get results, and it's an obligation I don't take lightly.

So if you're the owner or manager of a small or mid-sized business and you're serious, really serious, about taking your business to the next level and beyond, pick up the phone and give me a call. I'll be happy to discuss with you your business potential and goals, and see if we could work well together.

Thanks again for reading this book. If you like what you heard today, I promise that you will love working with me and TriFecta Marketing. If you would like to speak with me about your business development marketing potential and achieving exponential growth in your business, or if you have any questions at all, pick up the phone and give me a call at (225) 308-3323. Or send me an email at Russ@RussHolder.com.

About Russ Holder

Russ Holder is a leading business development and marketing expert and best-selling author with the life purpose of "helping companies systematically and dramatically accelerate their growth."

Through his books, speaking engagements, and consulting programs, Russ has served as a strategic advisor to leaders of high-growth businesses worldwide, including multiple members of both the Fortune and Inc. 500 lists. As the CEO and founder of TriFecta Marketing, a results-driven business development and marketing firm, Russ has helped over 200 entrepreneurs and business leaders in 40-plus industries and professions increase sales, profits and market share.

Maximizing Business Growth was published in 2010 and was an Amazon Best Seller. Based on Russ's proprietary TriFecta Exponential Growth Model, the book focuses on systematically improving the Nine Growth Keys of a business to generate powerful Marketing Synergy and exponential growth.

Visit Russ Holder on the web at www.RussHolder.com.

Russ Holder's business development and marketing strategies have been tested worldwide for almost 20 years. With client companies ranging from small, one-person operations to some of the most successful Fortune 500 corporations, Russ's methods, systems and strategies eliminate the guesswork and financial risk associated with marketing and growing your business.

More Books by Russ Holder

Growing Your Business During an Economic Meltdown (2007–ISBN: 978-1-939315-16-8)

Get 'Em and Keep 'Em (2008-ISBN: 978-1-939315-15-1)

Points of Failure (2009–ISBN: 978-1-939315-17-5)

Maximizing Business Growth (2010–ISBN: 978-1-939315-01-4)

20 Reasons Why Your Sales Stink (2012–ISBN: 978-1-939315-02-1)

Going Up (2014–ISBN: 978-1-939315-14-4)

IMPORTANT NOTE: The information in this book only scratches the surface of getting the best results from your sales and marketing efforts. Be sure to get on Russ Holder's mailing list for up-to-date information and resources to grow your business in sales, profits and market share. You can sign up at www.RussHolder.com.